First Edition
Genuine Autographed Collectible

Do you want me to sign it in ink or in lipstick?

BE ART
YOU ARE BORN FOR GREATNESS
YOU ARE A MASTERPIECE

Gift Card

Date:

To:

From:

Message:

What Do Books Do?
BOOKS ARE POWERFUL

Books Educate!
Books Enlighten!
Books Empower!
Books Emancipate!
Books Entertain!
Books Spring Eternal!
Books Drive Exploration!
Books Spark Evolution!
Books Ignite Revolution!

Sharon Esther Lampert

The Awesome Art of Alliteration Using One Letter of the Alphabet
Gift Shop: BooksArePowerful.com

UNLEASH THE CREATOR THE GOD WITHIN

10 Esoteric Laws of Genius and Creativity

Self-Help, Art, Creativity, Education, God, Genius, Sharon Esther Lampert

UNLEASH THE CREATOR THE GOD WITHIN
10 Esoteric Laws of Genius and Creativity

©2023 @2022 by Sharon Esther Lampert. All Rights Reserved. No part of this book may be used or reproduced in any manner whatsoever without written permission except in the case of brief quotations embodied in critical articles and reviews.

KADIMAH PRESS: GIFTS OF GENIUS books may be purchased for education, business, or sales promotional use.

ISBN Hardcover: 978-1-885872-21-0
ISBN Paperback: 978-1-885872-22-7
ISBN E-Book: 978-1-885872-23-4
Library of Congress Catalog Card Number: 2015906114

FAN MAIL:
Website: www.SharonEstherLampert.com
Email: FANS@SharonEstherLampert.com

For Global Online Orders and Distribution:
INGRAM 1 Ingram Blvd. La Vergne, TN 37086-3629
Phone: 615-793-5000, Fax orders: 615-287-6990

Book Design and Interior: Sharon Esther Lampert

Editor: Dave Segal

First Edition

Manufactured in the United States of America

UNLEASH THE CREATOR THE GOD WITHIN

10 Esoteric Laws of Genius and Creativity

KADIMAH PRESS
Gifts of Genius

What Happens When You Dress Up Albert Einstein as Marilyn Monroe?

SHARON ESTHER LAMPERT

Dedication

Unleash The Creator The God Within

I was born gifted. My inherited gift is a gift that keeps giving...

I refer to my extra-body part as my "Creative Apparatus."

My gift is my most important relationship, my most rewarding relationship, and paradoxically, my most difficult relationship:

EXCITING!   EXHILERATING!   ELECTRIFYING!   EXHAUSTING!

I awake in the middle of a sleepless night, and write the whole book! There are no rough drafts!

I am no longer an I — I am a WE — Maybe a THEY!

My gift did not come with an instruction manual. There were no teachers to guide me, and no classes to teach how to maximize my creative potential. Artistic **intuitive gifts of** insight, imagination, **and** vision cannot be taught in school. It is a feeling — not a fact.

I am its servant and messenger, and the instrument of its desires and destiny!

Sharon Esther Lampert

SEE THE WORLD THROUGH THE EYES OF A CREATIVE GENIUS

Poet, **P**hilosopher, **P**rophet, **P**eacemaker, **P**rincess & **P**ea, **P**aladin of Education, and **Pr**o**di**gy

V.E.S.S.E.L. Very. Extra. Special. Sharon. Esther. Lampert.

#1 Poetry Website for Student Projects
The Greatest Poems Ever Written on Extraordinary World Events

True Love

True Love is Unconditional.
True Love is Found in the Deed.
True Love is Found in the We.
True Love Joins the Heart,
Mind, and Body as One.

By Sharon Esther Lampert

**The Sole Intention of My Poetry
is to Add LIGHT to Your Soul
Sharon Esther Lampert**

**Food is for the Body
Education is for the Mind
Poetry is for the Soul
Sharon Esther Lampert**

"A good poem is a contribution to reality. The world is never the same once a good poem has been added to it. A good poem helps to change the shape of the universe, helps to extend everyone's knowledge of himself and the world around him."
—Dylan Thomas

Unleash The Creator The GOD Within

#1 Poetry Website for Student Projects

POE**T**REE

Ink needs a Pen
Pen needs Paper
Paper needs a Poem
Poem needs a Poet
Poet needs a Muse
Muse needs a Poet
Poet needs Divine Inspiration
Divine Inspiration needs Divine Intervention
Divine Intervention needs Divine Grace
Divine Grace needs Immortality
Immortality needs Eternity
Eternity needs Readers of Poetry

By Sharon Esther Lampert

@All Rights Reserved. Sharon Esther Lampert.

Just because Creativity is Mystical doesn't mean it shouldn't also be Demystified...

Elizabeth Gilbert

V.E.S.S.E.L. Very. Extra. Special. Sharon. Esther. Lampert.

Table of Contents

Introduction
p. 1

10 Esoteric Laws of Genius and Creativity
5 Parts — 10 Elements

Part 1
Element 1
The Artist and Artwork Become One
1st Esoteric Law of Creativity
V.E.S.S.E.L.
p. 3

Element 2
2nd Esoteric Law of Creativity
INSPIRATION
p. 9

Element 3
3rd Esoteric Law of Creativity
IMPREGNATION
p. 13

Element 4
4th Esoteric Law of Creativity
INCUBATION
p. 17

Part 2
Element 5
The Artist and Artwork Separate into Two
5th Esoteric Law of Creativity
GENESIS

Part 3

Element 6

The Artist

6th Esoteric Law of Creativity

SILENT:LISTEN

p. 25

Part 4

Element 7

The Artwork

7th Esoteric Law of Creativity

METAMORPHOSIS

p. 29

Element 8

8th Esoteric Law of Creativity

REVELATION

p. 33

Element 9

9th Esoteric Law of Creativity

SIGNATURE

p. 41

Part 5

Element 10

The Artist is Mortal. The Artwork is Immortal

10th Esoteric Law of Creativity

IMMORTALITY

p. 45

APPENDIX

About the Prodigy ... pp. 49-53
FAN MAIL ... pp. 54-60
POETRY SEX SCANDAL at Barnes & Noble ... p. 61
Kadimah Press: Gifts of Genius ... pp. 63-64
Thank You ... p. 65
One of the World's Greatest Poets ... p. 66
World Famous Quotes ... p. 67

INTRODUCTION

Revelations! My Books Write Themselves!

"Did you write this all by yourself?" asks an ardent fan seated in the audience of an open-mic poetry reading. "Yes," I reply emphatically, "I stole all of the words from the dictionary!" (His question is a sexiest microaggression).

"I read your entire website, and it is brilliant!" Exclaims another ardent fan and friend of many years.

"Who is your inner genie?" is another question I am often asked.

One evening, at a poetry reading, a crushed-up white piece of paper was sent from the back of the room to the front, similar to passing a note in grade school behind a teacher's back, and it said the following: "The Spirit of God is Inside You!"

I do have four books with God in the title! One book is, "God Talks to Me: A Working Definition of God." I am a BOOK MOMMY with 40+ BOOK BABIES!

Every month, I get busy printing out my pocket poems to hand out to people that I meet on NYC buses and subways, and in NYC stores and restaurants. "Would you like a gift of poetry?" I ask. The answer is always, "Yes, thank you for the poetry!" Poetry is a great way to make new friends and fans. Most often, I hear that my poem is posted on a fan's refrigerator door. Great spot!

One afternoon, while riding a NYC public bus, I hand out some pocket poems to the passengers seated on the right and left of me.

Within a NY minute, one of the passengers on the bus asks me for more of my pocket poems. She walks up and down the aisle of the bus, and hands out my pocket poems to every person on the bus. It is a very big compliment, and I thank her profusely!

On my annual trip to the dentist's office, the dental-office assistant asks me for more pocket poems, and hands them out to the doctors and patients in the waiting room — and again, I thank her immensely.

On my annual trip for a medical checkup, I recall while prepping for a medical exam, the doctor pulling out a pocket poem from his wallet to let me know that he received the gift of poetry while on vacation at a Caribbean resort. "Is it you?" he asks. The poem is titled, "The Restless Sunrise."

"Yes!" I confirm.

I was so happy to hear that my pocket poetry had taken flight and was traveling the world, even if I, the poet, was grounded, locked away in a tiny-studio apartment, ball and chain to a iMAC APPLE computer, for what seemed like a decade of prolific creativity in poetry, philosophy, theology, and education.

There is a tall and lanky man who frequently reads his own poetry at our monthly open-mic poetry event. Whenever he sees me — he reminds me — that whenever he visits his father's gravesite, he reads my poem, "The 22 Commandments" to his beloved father of blessed memory. I am honored!

BE ART

YOU ARE A MASTERPIECE!
YOU ARE BORN FOR GREATNESS!

Sharon Esther Lampert

> Don't bend; don't water it down;
> don't try to make it logical;
> don't edit your own soul according
> to the fashion. Rather, follow your
> most intense obsessions mercilessly.
>
> — Franz Kafka

Part 1 — Element 1
The Artist and The Artwork Become One
1st Esoteric Law of Creativity

V.E.S.S.E.L.

Very. Extra. Special. Sharon. Esther Lampert.

> Every child is an artist. The problem is how
> to remain an artist once he grows up.
>
> Pablo Picasso

My father Abraham Lampert's nickname was

BEZALEL
"In the Shadow of God"

the Chief Architect of the Ark of the Covenant.
I Inherited the Blessing.

Sharon Esther Lampert

V.E.S.S.E.L.
Very. Extra. Special. Sharon. Esther. Lampert.

Exodus 31:1-3, 5 Books of Moses
1. Then the Lord spoke to Moses, saying:
2. "See, I have called by name **BEZALEL** the son of Uri, the son of Hur, of the tribe of Judah.
3. And I have filled him with the Spirit of God, in wisdom, in understanding, in knowledge, and in all manner of workmanship.

V.E.S.S.E.L. Very. Extra. Special. Sharon. Esther. Lampert.

Part 1 — Element 1
The Artist and The Artwork Become One
1st Esoteric Law of Creativity

V.E.S.S.E.L.
Very. Extra. Special. Sharon. Esther. Lampert.

Artistic gifts are inherited. I was one of the lucky ones! I was born with an extra-body part, a "Creative Apparatus." I inherited artistic gifts from the maternal and paternal sides of my family.

My maternal grandfather Benjamin Paikoff was a painter, and made his living as a sign painter. My grandfather decorated the hallways of his house with his paintings (see next page).

My father Abraham Lampert was a sculptor, and made his living as a handyman and carpenter. My father's Cyprus stone Shabbat candlesticks sculpture was on exhibit in the Museum of Jewish Heritage, NYC, USA (see next page).

At the age of 9, my MOMMY wrote me a note that she left on my desk in my bedroom:

"THE QUEEN HAS ARRIVED!
My daughter is a poet, philosopher, and teacher!
You are the Princess and the Pea! Beauty & Brains!"
MOMMY, XOXO

At age 9, I was writing books on memo pads, and binding them together with a stapler. No one ever said, "Sharon is a publisher!" My books were educational in nature. I was passionately attached to my cat, and wrote self-help books on taking care of my cat. I also cared for meandering cats strolling through my backyard — every cat got an ear wash, a knited-cat collar, and a meal. Years later, my cat SCHMALTZY became a a world famous piano-playing virtuoso! SCHMALTZY.com

During my childhood, I had a subscription to a monthly art-project club. I would create all kinds of art projects, and decorate my room with my own creations.

I was born to create and educate!

Unleash The Creator The GOD Within

Lessons Learned & Bonus Material

1. **V.E.S.S.E.L. Very. Extra. Special. Sharon. Esther. Lampert.**
2. Genetics: Sharon Esther inherited artistic gifts from both parents: Maternal Grandfather Benjamin Paikoff was a painter. Sharon's father Abraham Lampert was a sculptor.
3. Sharon Esther's extra-body part is a "Creative Apparatus."
4. Sharon Esther wakes up in the middle of the night and writes the whole book!
   Sharon Esther has four books with God in the title.
5. The IDEA of Sharon Esther was conceived of in ISRAEL. Her mother traveled to ISRAEL from the USA. Her father traveled to ISRAEL from Russia. They met in ISRAEL. Sharon Esther was born in Brooklyn, NYC, and raised in the Rockaways, Queens, and lived her life in Manhattan, NYC, USA.

Favorite Quotes

"Beware when God lets loose a thinker on this planet."
—**Ralph Waldo Emerson**

"That brain of mine is something more than merely mortal, as time will show."
—**Ada Lovelace**

"There are preogatives of genius; to know without having learned; to draw just conclusion from unknown premises; to discern the soul of all things."
—**Ambrose Bierce**

"Who can unravel the essence, the stamp of the artistic temperament! Who can grasp the deep, instinctual fusion of discipline and dissipation on which it rests."
—**Thomas Mann, Death of Venice**

"Where the statue stood of Newton with his prism and silent face, the marble index of a mind forever voyaging through strange seas of thought, alone."
—**William Wordsworth**

V.E.S.S.E.L. Very. Extra. Special. Sharon. Esther. Lampert.

Artistic Gifts Are Inherited
I Inherited Two Sets of Artistic Genes

My Maternal Grandfather
Benjamin Paikoff
PAINTER

My Maternal Grandfather
Born in Belarussia – Immigrated to Brooklyn NYC, USA
Escaped Anti-Semitic Russian Pogroms
Wall Painting in Hallway of House
Winthrop Street, Brooklyn NYC, USA

Unleash The Creator The GOD Within

My Father Abraham Lampert
SCULPTOR

Born in Russia – Israeli Citizen 10 Years – U.S.A. Citizen
Sole Survivor of Family During the Holocaust
Exhibit: Museum of Jewish Heritage, NYC, USA
Made in Jewish Internment Camps in Cyprus
Made of Cyprus Stone

When you are inspired by some great
purpose, some extraordinary project,
all your thoughts break their bonds;
your mind transcends limitations;
your conscious expands in every direction;
and you find yourself in a great,
new and wonderful world.

Patanjali
Hindu, India, 2nd Century

Part 1 — Element 2

The Artist and The Artwork Become One
2nd Esoteric Law of Creativity

INSPIRATION

Creativity defies precise definition.
This conclusion does not bother me at all.
In fact, I am quite happy with it.
Creativity is almost infinite.
It involves every sense – sight, smell,
hearing, feeling, taste and even
perhaps the extrasensory.
Much of it is unseen,
nonverbal and unconscious.
Therefore, even if we had a precise
concept of creativity, I am certain we would
have difficulty putting it into words.

- E, Paul Torrance, 1998
"Father of Creativity"

The artist is
a receptacle
for emotions
that come from
all over the place:
from the sky,
from the earth,
from a scrap of paper,
from a passing shape,
from a spider's web.

Pablo Picasso

V.E.S.S.E.L. Very. Extra. Special. Sharon. Esther. Lampert.

Part 1 — Element 2
The Artist and The Artwork Become One
2nd Esoteric Law of Creativity

INSPIRATION

Everything in my environment is going to get processed through my extra-body part, a "Creative Apparatus" — and will either become a poem, a prophecy, a philosophy or an educational manifesto. **EVERYTHING IS INSPIRATION**!

I am an OLD SOUL — I was never young! I am a lefty. As a gifted V.E.S.S.E.L., I live on a unique emotional "frequency," that I describe as feeling like being a high strung through-bred racehorse. The people around me experience it, and often remark, "Sharon is so intense!" The words, "So intense!" have followed me around since childhood.

As I was born at the dawn of the Digital Revolution, and the birth of the internet so I had the deft advantage of Googling the word, "Creative Genius." I was delighted to find the website: www.creativegenius.org. The very first sentence is, "Creative Geniuses exhibit very high levels of emotional intensity."

Well, for the very first time, I was able to make sense of it for myself, and for those around me. Sometimes, I introduce myself by asking a question, "Have you ever met a creative genius?" Most people reply, "No!" I then explain that, "I am a creative genius, and exhibit very high levels of emotional intensity." This introduction has been very helpful to me. It builds a bridge of understanding and respect.

INSPIRATION comes in the form of MUSES. I have been fortunate to have MUSES appear and disappear, and leave an ARTWORK on their way out — as I hum the words to the song, **"Give me a KISS to build a dream on, and my imagination will thrive upon that KISS..."**

In less than a NY minute, a KISS from a MUSE can create an immortal work of art.

I am IMPRENATED!

An ARTWORK will be conceived in a NY minute!

Unleash The Creator The GOD Within

Lessons Learned & Bonus Material

1. EVERYTHING IS INSPIRATION!
2. Sharon Esther's extra-body part, a "CREATIVE APPARATUS" transforms the world into works of art.
3. Sharon lives on a unique artistic "FREQUENCY."
4. Creative geniuses exhibit very high levels of "EMOTIONAL INTENSITY."
5. "You are so intense!" is a common observation.
6. Sharon is a lefty — a commmon trait among artists.
7. A MUSE births an ARTWORK with a KISS.
8. Sharon's book, "CUPID" was birthed by a KISS.

Favorite Quotes

"In every man of genius, a strange force is brought into the world."
—Havellock Ellis

"No one was ever great without some portion of divine inspiration."
—Marcus Tullius Cicero

"Genius finds its own road and lights its own lamp."
—Robert Aris Willmott

"Ideas come from everything."
—Alfred Hitchcock

"A new idea is delicate. It can be killed by a sneer or a yawn; it can be stabbed to death by a quip and worried to death by a frown on the right man's brow."
—Charles Brower

"Genius is one percent inspiration and ninty-nine perspiration."
—Thomas A. Edison

> If you're an artist,
> art will find you!
>
> Pamela Anderson
> Sex Symbol,
> TV & Broadway Star

Part 1 — Element 3

The Artist and The Artwork Become One
3rd Esoteric Law of Creativity

IMPREGNATION

> You Don't Choose Art.
> Art Chooses You.
>
> Unknown

"The deepest experience of the creator is feminine, for it is experience of receiving and bearing."

Rainer Maria Rilke

V.E.S.S.E.L. Very. Extra. Special. Sharon. Esther. Lampert.

Part 1 — Element 3

The Artist and The Artwork Become One
3rd Esoteric Law of Creativity

IMPREGNATION

When the Marvel superhero Spider-Man gets bit by a spider and undergoes a transformation from a science student to a superhero with unique powers who can impact the world with his special gifts — this IMPREGNATION of the spider's venon within his body best illustrates how an ARTIST (V.E.S.S.E.L.) feels when INSPIRATIONS IMPREGNATE the ARTIST.

Our mind, thoughts, and ideas are **metaphysical** — invisible and intangible entities — beyond the scope of scientific inquiry. Our mind consists of the **subconscious mind** and the **conscious mind**.

The INSPIRATIONS exist in the world as intangible and invisible vibrations that infiltrate the ARTIST's sensory apparatus — and take root in the **unconscious mind.**

The ARTIST had no idea that he or she was IMPREGNATED — nor had any choice in the matter. INSPIRATIONS commingle in the subconscious of an ARTIST (the messenger) and take on a life of its own — with its own inherent message, meaning and mission.

When the INSPIRATIONS reach the conscious mind, the ARTIST is inspired and creates an ARTWORK.

Fertilization is usually used to describe how a single sperm and a single egg commingle — and become implanted in a female's uterus. The female cannot consciously experience the fertilization into her uterus. Nor does the female have any control over whether the baby is a male or female — or what the child will look like.

Here too, the ARTIST cannot feel the IMPREGNATION into the **subconscious mind**. The ARTIST and ARTWORK have become one.

Unleash The Creator The GOD Within

Lessons Learned & Bonus Material

1. Physics is the laws of the universe.
2. Metaphysics is beyond the scope of scientific inquiry.
3. Metaphysics: The **subconscious and conscious mind** are invisible and intangible entities.
4. Metaphysics: **Ideas** in the **subconscious and conscious mind** are invisible and intangible entities.
5. An ARTIST is IMPREGNATED by invisible and intangible external INSPIRATIONS.
6. IMPREGNATION is an invisible and intangible external and internal process.
7. After IMPREGNATION, the ARTWORK becomes an invisible and intangible entity in the **unconscious mind.**
8. ARTWORKS in the **unconscious mind** travel to the **conscious mind** — like a fertilized egg in the uterus before it exits the womb into the world.

Favorite Quote

The future enters into us,
in order to transform itself
in us, long before it happens.

Rainer Maria Rilke

Part 1 — Element 4

The Artist and The Artwork Become One
4th Esoteric Law of Creativity

INCUBATION

Art is a collaboration between God and the artist, and the less the artist does the better.

Andre Gide

The definition of genius is that is acts unconsciously; and those who have pondered immortal works, have done so without knowing how or why. The greatest power operates unseen.

William Hazlitt

I dream of painting and then I paint my dream.

Vincent Van Gogh

V.E.S.S.E.L. Very. Extra. Special. Sharon. Esther. Lampert.

Part 1 — Element 4

The Artist and The Artwork Become One
4th Esoteric Law of Creativity

INCUBATION

My book, "Who Knew God Was Such a Chatterbox" was written in one night.

INCUBATION: Two years before, I had 10 words of the book ringing in my head. On January 31, 2021, the book was born. For me, my literary masterpieces are born whole. I have the gift of AUTOMATIC writing.

Similar to the 9-month birth of a baby, the INSPIRATIONS will INCUBATE in my metaphysical **unconscious mind**, and in time reach my **conscious mind**. The birth of my ARTWORKS gush like a spring of water — or an oil geyser from my **unconscious mind**.

Unlike the 9-month INCUBATION period of every human child ever born — each ARTWORK has its own unique gestation period.

The gift has a flaw — an annoying typo! I accept the gift's limitations. Like a baby who must be bathed after a birth — I must bathe my book — and find the annoying typo. I have trained my left brain to track down the annoying typo. This typo occurs when I shift gears, like in a car — from creative right brain to editorial left brain — or drive or park into reverse.

When I sit down at my APPLE MAC Book Pro computer to write, there are days when I have no choice as to what I will write that day — my books write themselves. As a V.E.S.S.E.L., I have written entire books in a single day. My book, SILLY LITTLE BOYS: 40 RULES OF MANHOOD was written in one day. The book is blue comedy! I had no idea that I would write that book! I love this book! I love all my books! I do have favorites!

Unleash The Creator The GOD Within

Lessons Learned & Bonus Material

1. **INSPIRATIONS IMPREGNATE** and **INCUBATE** in the **unconscious mind** — and travel to the **conscious mind**.

2. Each ARTWORK has its own INCUBATION period.

3. Sharon has no idea what book will be written next!

4. Sharon has the gift of AUTOMATIC writing. Sharon's books write themselves! ARTWORKS are written in one day — like a gushing oil geyser.

5. Sharon's ARTWORKS are born whole with an annoying typo. Sharon has trained her editorial-left brain to find and repair the annoying typo — just like a new baby that needs a bath after birth. **In fact, every living being needs a bath after birth!**

6. Sharon's creative-right brain sends her the correct word, but cannot spell the word. Her editorial-left brain is in charge of spelling the words.

7. Writing is a creative-right brain and editorial-left brain process.

Favorite Quote

Being an artist means, not reckoning and counting, but ripening like the tree, which does not force its sap and stands confident in the storms of spring without the fear that after them may come no summer.

Rainer Maria Rilke

Part 2 — Element 5
The Artist and The Artwork Become Two
5th Esoteric Law of Creativity
GENESIS

The highest endowments
do not create –
they merely discover.
All transcendent genius
has the power to make us
know this as utter truth.
Shakespeare, Beethoven,
it is inconceivable that they have
fashioned the works of their lives;
they saw and heard the universe
that is opaque and dumb to us.

Ruth Benedict

V.E.S.S.E.L. Very. Extra. Special. Sharon. Esther. Lampert.

Part 2 — Element 5
The Artist and The Artwork Become Two
5th Esoteric Law of Creativity

GENESIS

Every writer writes the exact same way — one word at a time. Every writer transforms a blank piece of paper — nothing into something.

Ideas in the **unconscious** and **conscious mind** are invisible and intangible metaphysical entities.

The first tool of a writer is **brainstorming** for **ideas**. A writer makes a list of **ideas** and then sorts the **ideas** into three groupings of good, bad, and great ideas. Good and bad ideas are discarded, and the great ideas remain, e.g., **Gold** is sorted out from the silver and the bronze. **Ideas** that arise in the metaphysical **conscious mind** are transferred to a blank piece of paper or typed into a personal computer.

As the words land on the blank page, the ARTIST and ARTWORK become two separate entities.

This is the beginning: the GENESIS of the life of the ARTWORK as a distinct entity of its own — with its own internal reason and rhyme for its existence.

The ARTIST will move on to other ARTWORKS, but each ARTWORK continues to exist in the world and takes up space in the world — and is on its own unique **mission**, e.g., Books are read by future generations.

GENESIS: The day, time, and weight a baby exits the womb is recorded. I always write down the date of my IDEA — even if I just have 10 words floating around in my conscious mind:

2018-2021: For 2 years, 10 words rang in my head:
"God Talks to Me, I am hungry! I am naked!"
2021: The book is birthed whole in one night:
January 31, 2021, from 1 a.m. - 10 a.m.

Unleash The Creator The GOD Within

Lessons Learned & Bonus Material

1. All writers write the exact same way — one word at a time.
2. All writers transform a blank piece of paper from nothing into something.
3. **GENESIS** is the moment the **ARTIST** and **ARTWORK** separate into two distinct — but related entities.
4. **ARTWORKS** live in the world with a unique destiny for eons into eternity. The **ARTIST** is the messenger.
5. **GENESIS:** Sharon Esther records the birth of her ideas and tracks their growth and maturation.

Favorite Quotes

"Creativity is always a leap of faith. You're faced with a blank page, blank easel, or an empty stage."
—Julia Cameron

"No matter what people tell you, words and ideas can change the world!"
—Robin Williams

"A library is the delivery room for the birth of ideas, a place where history comes to life."
—Norman Cousins

"Creativity is allowing yourself to make mistakes. Art is knowing which ones to keep."
—Scott Adams

"Creativity is seeing what others see and thinking what no one else ever thought."
—Albert Einstein

Be Still and Know That I Am God
Psalms 46:10

Part 3 — Element 6
The Artist
6th Esoteric Law of Creativity

SILENT:LISTEN

(metaphysical relationship: words share the same letters)

...because talent isn't genius, and no amount of energy can make it so. I want to be great, or nothing.

— Louisa May Alcott, Little Women

Silence is the language
God speaks. The rest is
a bad translation.

Thomas Keating

All true artists,
whether they
know it or not,
create from a place
of no-mind,
from inner stillness.

Eckhart Tolle

Who Knew God Was
Such a Chatterbox?

God Talks To Me
A Working Definition of God

GOD IS GO! DO!

Prophet Sharon Esther Lampert

V.E.S.S.E.L. **V**ery. **E**xtra. **S**pecial. **S**haron. **E**sther. **L**ampert.

Part 3 — Element 6
The Artist
6th Esoteric Law of Creativity

SILENT:LISTEN

(**meta**physical relationship: words share the same letters)

ART IS OF THE HEART
Sharon Esher Lampert   Giftshop: Artheart.store

My authors depend upon me to make the right artistic decisions for them. As an **ARTIST**, creative dexterity is an instinctual response — like my blinking eyelids.

"**Artistic Isolation**" is the term I have coined to describe the living conditions that are required to be able to maintain an environment of **SILENT** and intuitive **LISTENING**. "**IN THE ZONE**" is a popular term for the special place where the creative magic happens.

My authors are delighted to have access to my artistic gifts, and accept all of the creative decisions made on their behalf. Their books contain titles, subtitles, and book hooks that I have designed. They are forever grateful. Every book published is imprinted with my artistic vision.

When an **ARTWORK** is in its infancy, there are many creative decisions that need to be made:

Q. What size book?
Q. Color or black and white?
Q. What font for the headers and text?
Q. What is the title and subtitle?
Q. What book hook to engage the readers?
Q. Which photos and illustrations?

As an **ARTIST**, I am able to make the right artistic decisions because, **creative decisions are ensconced in FEELINGS not facts.** These sense perceptions cannot be taught in a school. These are gifts of **intuition, insight, imagination,** and **vision.**

Unleash The Creator The GOD Within

Lessons Learned & Bonus Material

1. The words SILENT and LISTEN share the same letters. They also share a metaphysical relation ship in message and meaning.
2. The words ART and HEART share a metaphysical relationship in message and meaning.
3. Artistic decisions are based in FEELINGS not facts.
4. "ARTISTIC ISOLATION" is necessary to create the right environment for "SILENT LISTENING!"
5. Artistic gifts of INTUITION, INSIGHT, IMAGINATION and VISION cannot be taught in school.

Favorite Quotes

"In **art**, the hand can never execute anything higher than the **heart** can inspire."
—**Ralph Waldo Emerson**

"I shut my eyes in order to see."
—**Paul Gauguin**

"Loneliness is Death; Solitude is Divine."
—**Sharon Esther Lampert**

"I need solitude for my writing; not 'like a hermit' — that wouldn't be enough — but like a dead man!"
—**Franz Kafka**

"When I am completely myself, entirely alone during the night when **I cannot sleep**, it is on such occasions that my ideas flow best and most abundantly."
—**Mozart** (e.g., The Prince & The Pea!)

"All men's miseries derive from not being able to sit in a quiet room alone."
—**Blaise Pascal**

Part 4 — Element 7

The Artwork

7th Esoteric Law of Creativity

METAMORPHOSIS

Message, Meaning, Maturity, and Mission
Messengers, Messiahs, and Mystics
Mystery, Magic, Miracle, and Masterpiece

Do not get swept away by all of
the information available, but rather,
focus on the "nowness" of an experience
and process what it's telling you
to discover hidden riches of wisdom.

Professor Ted Coons
NYU Physiological Psychology

*I saw the angel
in the marble,
and carved until
I set him free!*

Michelangelo

He who works with his hands is a laborer.
He who works with his hands and his head is
a craftsman. He who works with his hands
and his head, and his heart is an artist.

Francis of Assisi

You cannot teach auteurs
beyond craft because that
is an innate artistic quality.

Professor Karl Bardosh
NYU, Tisch School of the Arts

V.E.S.S.E.L. Very. Extra. Special. Sharon. Esther. Lampert.

Part 4 — Element 7
The Artwork
7th Esoteric Law of Creativity

METAMORPHOSIS
Message, Meaning, Magic, Maturity, and Mission

(1) As the **ARTIST**, I become one with the **ARTWORK**. (2) I was **INSPIRED**. (3) I was **IMPREGNATED**. (4) The **ARTWORK INCUBATED** inside of me. (5) **GENESIS:** The idea is birthed whole like a baby — there are no rough drafts. (6) I am engaged in **SILENT LISTENING.**

I am pregnant with prose. Like a crocus under the earth that pops up in the spring, an idea will appear from nowhere, and ask me — the **Messenger** — to give it life, and nurture it until it **METAMORPHOSIZES: Message, Meaning, Magic, Maturity,** and **Mission.**

I live on a unique **FREQUENCY**, so I can see the entire book before it is written — once it is transmitted from my **subconscious mind** to my **conscious mind**.

METAMORPHOSIS: I see the whole book — and I start designing the book cover by choosing the fonts, the photo, the illustrations, and by giving the book a title and subtitle. Next, I design and format the chapters. I add the copyright page, ISBN, and PCN library number.

I write the book inside of a formatted book. I do not transfer the book from a Microsoft Word document into a formatted book. **MAGIC! There are no rough drafts!** There is only a final draft with an irrational and annoying typo!

My editorial-left brain is trained to reread and revise over and over, and over again. Right and left brain collaborate as a team, **"Please don't let me die with a typo!"** I go on the hunt for the annoying typo! I find it! I always stop, and thank my left brain! My right brain creates effortlessly, and it is my editorial-left brain that has to be of service to my creative-right brain. I buy my left hand a gift of jewelry.

My editorial-left brain diligently labors until exhaustion sets in. **FOCUS!** Every minute of each day is in service to the **maturation** of my literary works.

Unleash The Creator The GOD Within

Lessons Learned & Bonus Material

1. **METAMORPHOSIS** is the cultivation of the **ARTWORK** in the hands of the **ARTIST**, the **m**essenger, until the **ARTWORK** reaches **m**aturity: **m**essage, **m**eaning, **m**agic, and **m**ission.

2. Sharon Esther lives on a unique **FREQUENCY,** and can see the entire book before it is written. She writes her books directly into a formatted book. Revelations! My Books Write Themselves! There are no rough drafts! Some books are written in one day or one night! **Exhausting!**

3. Sharon Esther trained her editorial-left brain to find the irrational and annoying typo!

Favorite Quotes

"We delight in the beauty of the butterfly, but rarely admit the changes it has gone through to achieve that beauty."
—Maya Angelou

"I cannot make you understand. I cannot make anyone understand what is happening inside me. I cannot even explain it to myself."
—Franz Kafka, **THE METAMORPHOSIS**

"Creativity is sacred, and it is not sacred. What we make matters enormously, and it doesn't matter at all. We toil alone, and we are accompanied by spirits. We are terrified, and we are brave. Art is a crushing chore and a wonderful privilege."
—Elizabeth Gilbert

"There are painters who transform the sun into a yellow spot, but there are others who, thanks to their art and intelligence, transform a yellow spot into the sun."
—Pablo Picasso

> "The aim of art is to represent not the outward appearance of things, but their inward significance."
> Aristotle

Part 4 – Element 8

The Artwork

8th Esoteric Law of Creativity

REVELATION

If nature can do it — why can't we?

Andrew Hamilton
NYU President and Professor of Chemistry

GOD IS GO! DO!
God Can Only Do For You What God Can Do Through You

God Is Not Physics — The Laws of the Universe!

God Is Metaphysics — Beyond Scientific Inquiry

An Invisible and Intangible Entity

Like Your Mind, Thoughts, and Ideas

SHARON ESTHER LAMPERT
SEE THE WORLD THROUGH THE EYES OF A CREATIVE GENIUS

Read My Book:
"Who Knew God Was Such a Chatterbox"

"Please remain true
to your calling, unimpeded
by those who may wish to
curb the freedom of your
expression or impose
limits on your imagination.

Enough said!

Let there be no squeaking
like mice about
your achievements,
but only roaring,
like a pride of lions."

Her Majesty
Queen Camilla Windsor
Reading Room Charity
February 3rd, 2023

V.E.S.S.E.L. Very. Extra. Special. Sharon. Esther. Lampert.

Part 4 — Element 8
The Artwork
8th Esoteric Law of Creativity

REVELATION

REVELATION is the moment the 10 words that have been ringing in my head for two years reveal their **m**essage, **m**eaning, and **m**ission to me.

Similar to birthing a baby, my book, "Who Knew God Was Such a Chatterbox" is born into the world. The book was born on January 31, 2021 at 1 a.m. — 10 a.m., weighing in at 80 pages.

The **REVELATION** contained in this book is:

GOD IS GO! DO!
God Can Only Do For You What God Can Do Through You!

Whenever I find myself at the local copy shop on 82nd Street in Manhatten on 3rd Avenue, I bump into my dear neighbor, Rabbi Ben Tzion Krasnianski of the Upper East Side Chabad Center. The Rabbi is also standing on line waiting to make copies (**meta**physical connection: we are in sync!)

We exchange a warm and friendly hello. What's always new in his life is that his wife has given birth to another baby — her 10th. **MAZAL TOV!**

What's always new in my life is that I have also given birth to another poetry or philosophy or education book. The Rabbi usually leaves the copy shop with one of my new poems. Rabbi Krasnianski is an ardent fan!

One Shabbat, I enter the Chabad House bearing gifts of poetry, "The 22 Commandments: All You Will Ever Need to Know About God." I wait impatiently for the Rabbi to stop talking — so I can hand out my poem. The Rabbi's last sentence is, "Inside every Jewish person is a little Moses trying to get out!" **What a great introduction!** I hand out my poem, "The 22 Commandments!" (**meta**physical connection: we are in sync!)

REVELATIONS: I have given birth to four books with the word **God** in the title. **MAZAL TOV!**

Unleash The Creator The GOD Within

Lessons Learned & Bonus Material

1. **REVELATION**: The **ARTWORK** is born with its own **m**essage, **m**eaning, and **m**ission.

2. **REVELATION**: The **ARTWORK** born into the mind of one **ARTIST** will live in the world, and communicate with other people in the world, and with future generations for eons into eternity.

3. Some of Sharon Esther's **REVELATIONS**:
   - FIGHT TO LIVE, LIVE TO FIGHT, BORN TO DIE
   - LONELINESS IS DEATH, SOLITUDE IS DIVINE
   - THERE IS ONLY ONE TRUTH, NO ONE HAS THE TRUTH
   - Food Is for the Body, Education Is for the Mind, and Poetry Is for the Soul
   - BE HARD ON A WOMAN ONLY WHEN MAKING LOVE TO HER!
   - There Are No Believers! There Are Make-Believers & Non-Believers!
   - GOD IS GO! DO! God Can Only Do For You What God Can Do Through You!
   - Women Have All the Power, But Have Never Learned How to Use It!

Favorite Quotes

"Revelation can be more perilous than revolution."
 —Vladimir Nabokov

"To send light into the darkness of men's hearts - such is the duty of the artist."
—Schumann

"If art is to nourish the roots of our culture, society must set the artist free to follow his vision wherever it takes him. We must never forget that art is not a form of propaganda; it is a form of truth."
—**President John F. Kennedy**

"The **SOLE** intention of my poetry is to add LIGHT to your **SOUL**."
—**Sharon Esther Lampert**

"A man of genius makes no mistakes. His errors are the portals of discovery."
—**James Joyce**

"Art is either plagiarism or revolution!"
—**Paul Gauguin**

Part 4 – Element 9
The Artwork
9th Esoteric Law of Creativity

SIGNATURE

*An artist is not
paid for his labor
but for his vision.*
James MacNeill Whistler

Genius is the ability
to see things invisible,
to manipulate things
intangible, to paint
things that have
no features.
Joseph Joubert

For I dipped into the future,
far as human eye could see,
saw the vision of the world,
and all the wonder
that would be.
Alfred Tennyson

V.E.S.S.E.L. Very. **E**xtra. **S**pecial. **S**haron. **E**sther. **L**ampert.

Part 4 — Element 9

The Artwork
9th Esoteric Law of Creativity

SIGNATURE

If you look at my ARTWORKS, you will see a thread interwoven into the tapestry that lets you know and recognize that the poem belongs to **Sharon Esther Lampert**.

My ARTWORKS bear my SIGNATURE.

Each of my ARTWORKS takes you on a cinematic journey though a historical event — and the last lines end with the REVELATION: the message, the meaning and the mission. Lines commingle poetry, philosophy, and comedy into one singular sentence. There are many intricate and interwoven layers of message and meaning.

I always autograph my poems for my ardent fans. My ardent fans send me fabulous emails about how beautiful and brilliant I am.

My MOMMY would be ecstatic, as she was the first one to let me know this at age 9, "THE QUEEN HAD ARRIVED!" I have also become buxom. My grandmother and mother had watermelon breasts — and good-fitting bras had to be ordered. At age 40, my breasts continue to develop — and may have reached maturity: 36DDD. OY VEY!

I wish MOMMY was alive to see EVERYTHING! MOMMY would say MAZAL TOV! — not OY VEY!

When I prepare to read my work at an open-mic poetry event, it takes me a long time to get myself into the right mood to read my work. It always feels as if I am reading my poem for the very first time — I can't remember writing the poem! I see that my name is on the poem. I see that there is a photo of me on the poem.

Yes, I wrote the poem, but AUTOMATIC WRITING is faster than the speed of light! — I can't pass a test on my own work!

Unleash The Creator The GOD Within

Lessons Learned & Bonus Material

1. The **V.E.S.S.E.L.** and **INSPIRATIONS** become one. After **GENESIS**, they separate into two. The **ARTWORK** has its own meaning, message, and mission — yet bears the fingerprint and **SIGNATURE** of the **ARTIST**.

2. Sharon Esther's **SIGNATURE** is as follows:
   (1) To commingle poetry, philosophy, and comedy into a single sentence: **WORLD POETRY RECORD**
   (2) Condensation: Condense 5000 years of history into one page of poetry.
   (3) The **A**wesome **A**rt of **A**lliteration: 6 Books.
   (4) To write a poem or a whole book in one night.
   (5) The greatest poems ever written on extraordinary world events. #1 **Poetry Website for Student Projects**.
   (6) Transform F students into A students: **SMARTGRADES.**

3. Sharon Esther has the gift of **AUTOMATIC WRITING** (faster than the speed of light!). Sharon Esther can't remember writing her books — and she can't pass a test on her own literary works!

Favorite Quotes

"What you are, you are by accident of birth; what I am, I am by myself. There are and will be a thousand princes; there is only one Beethoven."
—**Ludwig van Beethoven**

"Success is when your signature becomes an autograph."
—**Abdul Kalam**

"Every artist dips his brush in his own soul, and paints his own nature into his pictures."
—**Henry Ward Beecher**

"The postman wants an autograph. The cab driver wants a picture. The waitress wants a handshake. Everyone wants a piece of you."
—**John Lennon**

Part 5 — Element 10
The Artist is Mortal. The Artwork Is Immortal.
10th Esoteric Law of Creativity

IMMORTALITY

Don't think about making art, just get it done. Let everyone else decide if it's good or bad, whether they love it or hate it. While they are deciding, make even more art.

Andy Warhol

"If your daily life seems poor,

do not blame it;

blame yourself that

you are not poet enough

to call forth its riches;

for the Creator

there is no poverty."

Rainer Maria Rilke

V.E.S.S.E.L. Very. Extra. Special. Sharon. Esther. Lampert.

Part 5 — Element 10
The Artist is Mortal. The Artwork Is Immortal.
10th Esoteric Law of Creativity

IMMORTALITY

April is poetry month in NYC — and there is a special day designated as, **"Poetry in Your Pocket Day."** On this day, you fill your pockets with poems, and share them with family, friends, and fans.

Every month, the bookstore Barnes & Noble has an open-mic poetry event. I enjoy reading my poems out loud. I always hand out copies of my poems to the audience (see my YouTube videos).

IMMORTALITY: One evening, I decide to read an erotic poem, "Shaddayim," and the manager of the Barnes and Noble bookstore sends me a, **"Cease and Desist"** letter, to stop me from reading my erotic poems, and to stop me from handing out my erotic poems to the audience.

I was thrilled to receive the letter and wrote an article, **"POETRY SEX SCANDAL AT BARNES & NOBLE."** I sent the manager of the store a "Thank you note." Scandals are good for poetry, publicity, and **IMMORTALITY.** My YouTube video is racking up **"LIKES."**

I call the corporate headquarters for intervention. The corporate office returns my call, and let's me know that I can return to the open-mic poetry event, read my erotic poems, and hand out copies to the audience. There will be no censorship of my erotic poems at the bookstore!

The Digital Revolution, internet, and email make it easy to send a poem to an English teacher in Mongolia — or to anyone anywhere in the world. Students are using my poems for their student projects. I receive lots of fan mail!

IMMORTALITY: Eventually, I am listed online as one of the world's greatest poets:
http://famouspoetsandpoems.com/poets.html

Unleash The Creator The GOD Within

Lessons Learned & Bonus Material

1. **ARTIST** is mortal. **ARTWORK** is immortal.
2. The Digital Revolution leveled the playing field by giving **ARTISTS** a global platform to share their **ARTWORKS** with a global audience.
3. Sharon Esther Lampert is listed online as one of the world's greatest poets:
   http://famouspoetsandpoems.com/poets.html

Favorite Quotes

"Of all the wonders that the world had to offer, only art promised immortality."
—Sergei Diaghilev

"The poets' scrolls will outlive the monuments of stone. Genius survives; all else is claimed by death."
—Edmund Spenser

"Life is short — the art long."
—Hippocrates

I don't want to achieve immortality through my work. I want to achieve it through not dying.
—Woody Allen

"IMMORTALITY IS MINE!"
—Sharon Esther Lampert

"I paint flowers so they will not die!"
—Frida Kahlo

"Immortality is the genius to move others long after you yourself have stopped moving."
—Frank Rooney

10 Esoteric Laws of Genius and Creativity

by Sharon Esther Lampert

I must study politics and war that my sons may have liberty to study mathematics and philosophy. My sons ought to study mathematics and philosophy, geography, natural history, naval architecture, navigation, commerce, and agriculture, in order to give their children a right to study painting, poetry, music, architecture, statuary, tapestry, and porcelain.

—USA President John Adams, 1780

Learn the rules like a pro, so you can break them like an artist.

Pablo Picasso

In a period of human history characterized by increasing alienation and identity crisis, some of the arts still retain and assert the possibilities of honest expression and human freedom.

Professor Laurin Raiken
NYU, Gallatin

Art is art, isn't it?
And water is water and east is east and west is west and if you take cranberries and stew them like apple-sauce they taste much more like prunes than rhubarb does.

Groucho Marx

Student Projects

1. List & Define: "10 Esoteric Laws of Genius and Creativity"

2. **Write an Essay** (3-5 pages)
   Choose one "Esoteric Law of Genius and Creativiy" and give an example showcasing an artist and artwork?

3. **Write a Research Paper** (5-8 pages)
   Read an artist's autobiography.
   Explore the creation of an artwork.
   Apply the "10 Esoteric Laws of Genius and Creativity"
   Use research—cite 5 primary sources.

4. **Keep a Daily Journal of Creative Ideas:**

UNLEASH THE CREATOR THE GOD WITHIN

a. Develop an awareness of your own artistic extra body part of a **"Creative Apparatus"** — **I**nsight, **I**ntuition, **I**magination, and **V**ision.

b. How does your **"Creative Apparatus"** prefer to communicate: writing, painting, sculpture, singing, photography, filmmaker, architecture, engineering, fashion, beauty, cooking, gardening, fashion, home decoration, or other.

c. **Plan in Place on Paper:** Develop your ideas by first writing them down on paper. Follow it up with concrete steps that will manifest your **VISION** into reality.

d. **Metamorphosis**: Let your creative ideas unfold organically — like a bud about to bloom into a rose. Use dates to keep track of the birth of your Ideas.
Birth of Idea: Date: Time:

Unleash The Creator The GOD Within
10 Esoteric Laws of Genius and Creativity

5 Parts — 10 Elements

BE ART
You Are Born for Greatness!
You Are a Masterpiece!

SHARON ESTHER LAMPERT
SEE THE WORLD THROUGH THE
EYES OF A CREATIVE GENIUS

Shop Global Bookstores
ISBN: Hardcover: 978-1-885872-21-0
ISBN: Paperback: 978-1-885872-22-7
ISBN: E-Book: 978-1-885872-23-4

Part 1
Element 1
The Artist and Artwork Become One
1st Esoteric Law of Creativity
VESSEL

Element 2
2nd Esoteric Law of Creativity
INSPIRATION

Element 3
3rd Esoteric Law of Creativity
IMPREGNATION

Element 4
4th Esoteric Law of Creativity
INCUBATION

Part 2
Element 5
The Artist and Artwork Become Two
5th Esoteric Law of Creativity
GENESIS

Part 3
Element 6
The Artist
6th Esoteric Law of Creativity
SILENT:LISTEN

Part 4
Element 7
The Artwork
7th Esoteric Law of Creativity
METAMORPHOSIS

Element 8
8th Esoteric Law of Creativity
REVELATION

Element 9
9th Esoteric Law of Creativity
SIGNATURE

Part 5
Element 10
The Artist is Mortal, The Artist is Immortal
10th Esoteric Law of Creativity
IMMORTALITY

About the Prodigy
SHARON ESTHER LAMPERT

**Talent hits a target
no one else can hit;
Genius hits a target
no one else can see!**
Arthur Schopenhauer

**Everywhere I go
I find a poet has been
there before me.**
Sigmund Freud

What Is Art?

**Art is the expression of the
soul of a human being.
When art moves you,
one soul has reached out
to touch another.**

SHARON ESTHER LAMPERT
SEE THE WORLD THROUGH THE EYES OF A CREATIVE GENIUS
www.SharonEstherLampert.com

SEE THE WORLD THROUGH THE EYES OF A CREATIVE GENIUS

NYU

Honored Sharon Lampert with an Award for
Multi-Interdisciplinary Studies
(YOUTUBE video)

- Prodigy
- Prophet
- Philosopher
- Poet
- Peacemaker
- Princess & Pea
- **PINUP**
- Performer: Vocalist
- Player: Jock
- Paladin of Education
- **PHOTON SUPERHERO**
- Princess Kadimah
- President
- Publisher
- Producer
- Psychobiologist
- Piano-Playing Cat
- Phoenix

Websites:
- SharonEstherLampert.com
- PhilosopherQueen.com
- WorldFamousPoems.com
- PoetryJewels.com
- GodIsGoDo.com
- Schmaltzy.com
- TrueLoveBurnsEternal.com
- SillyLittleBoys.com
- WinAtThin.com
- WomenHaveAllThePower.com
- WritersRunTheWorld.com
- BooksArePowerful.com
- HappyGrandparenting.com

Education:
SMARTGRADES
BRAIN POWER REVOLUTION
- Smartgrades.com
- EverydayanEasyA.com
- PhotonSuperHero.com
- BooksNotBombs.com

Publisher:
- PalmBeachBookPublisher.com
- MiamiBookPublisher.com
- ArtBooksGlobal.com
- UniversityBookPublisher.com

Unleash The Creator The GOD Within

About the Prodigy

SHARON ESTHER LAMPERT

V.E.S.S.E.L. **V**ery. **E**xtra. **S**pecial. **S**haron. **E**sther. **L**ampert.

PRODIGY

- **UNLEASH THE CREATOR, THE GOD WITHIN**

10 Esoteric Laws of Genius and Creativity

The **A**wesome **A**rt of **A**lliteration Using One Letter of The **A**lphabet

POET — "A LIST"

Greatest Poems Ever Written on Extraordinary World Events
One of the World's Greatest Poets
POETRY WORLD RECORD: 120 Words of Rhyme

http://famouspoetsandpoems.com/poets.html

PROPHET

- **Who Knew God was Such a Chatterbox GOD IS GO! DO!**
- **The 22 Commandments: All You Will Ever Need to Know About GOD**

Universal Moral Compass For All People, For All Religions, For All Time

PHILOSOPHER QUEEN

- God of What? 11 Esoteric Laws of Inextricability
- Sperm Manifesto: 10 Rules for the Road
- Temporary Insanity — Written in Letter **S**
  We Are Building Our Lives on a **S**and Trap
- Women Have All the Power But Have Never Learned How to Use It

PEACEMAKER

World Peace Equation.com

PHOTON SUPERHERO OF EDUCATION
PALADIN OF EDUCATION

SMARTGRADES BRAIN POWER REVOLUTION

- "The Silent Crisis Destroying America's Brightest Minds"
- EVERYDAY AN EASY A.com
- 40 Universal Gold Standards of Education
- 15 Stepping Stones of Academic Successs
- 15 Stumbling Blocks of Academic Failure

PRINCESS & PEA

- **SILLY LITTLE BOYS**: 40 Rules of Manhood - For Men of All Ages
- **C**UPID: **The Language of Love** — Written in Letter **C**
- **D**ESTINY: **D**ARE TO **D**REAM — Written in Letter **D**
- **P**ublish: The Secret Sauce of Book Sales — Written in Letter **P**
- Win at Thin: Fat Me, Skinny Me — Written in Letter **A**
- Love You More Than Yesterday — 14 Relationship Strategies for
  Happily Ever After

PINUP
SEXIEST CREATIVE GENIUS IN HUMAN HISTORY!

V.E.S.S.E.L. Very. Extra. Special. Sharon. Esther. Lampert.

Artists March to the Beat of a Different Drummer
Sharon Esther Lampert Marches to the Beat of an Entire Orchestra

Poet, **P**hilosopher, **P**rophet, **P**eacemaker, **P**rodigy
Paladin of Education, **P**HOTON SUPERHERO
Princess & **P**ea, **P**INUP, **P**hoenix

Blue-Eyed. **B**rilliant. **B**eautiful. **B**uxom. **B**ooks. **B**lessed.

Sharon Esther Lampert was born an **OLD SOUL** — She was never young!
    Sharon is a lefty, a common trait among artists.
    At age nine, Sharon was writing books on memo pads, and binding them together with a stapler.
    At age nine, her mother declared: "My daughter is a poet, philosopher, and teacher — **THE QUEEN HAS ARRIVED!**" She nicknamed her daughter, "The **P**rincess and the **P**ea!" Sharon's greatest literary works woke her up in the middle of the night — and made her get up out of bed — and write them down. Sharon writes a whole book in one day or one night!
    Sharon's mother was the sole person in Sharon's life who knew who she was from the **INSIDE OUT** — and what would become of her. Her beloved mother also knew to her very last breath... the exact day and, to the minute when she would die! (Eve Paikoff Lampert: June 3, 1925 — May 5, 1985).

Sharon Esther's Gifts Are Metaphysical — Beyond the Scope of Scientific Inquiry

There Are No Rough Drafts! — The Books Write Themselves!
(There Are 4 Books with GOD in the Title)

The Awesome Art of Alliteration Using One Letter of the Alphabet
C, S, D, E, F, T, and P

"A LIST" Sharon Esther Lampert is One of the World's Greatest Poets
http://famouspoetsandpoems.com/poets.html

#1 Poetry Website for Student Projects
    On a global scale, Sharon's poetry is used by teachers for their poetry lesson plans, and by students for their school projects.

New York University Awards — (YOUTUBE videos) BA, MA, MA

Sharon Esther earned three degrees from NYU — and she was honored with two NYU awards. Sharon represented her class at her graduation — and was honored with an award for **"Multi-Interdisciplinary Studies."**
    Sharon also played on the NYU Women's Varsity Basketball Team as a **C**enter in the $16-million Coles Sports Center.
    Sharon won an "NYU Weightlifting Contest" — Sharon was the sole contestant — so she won! (NYU Washington Square Newspaper article).

#1 Poetry Website
For Student Projects

FAN MAIL
POET@WORLDFAMOUSPOEMS.COM

Sharon@SharonEstherLampert.com

V.E.S.S.E.L. Very. Extra. Special. Sharon. Esther. Lampert.

FAN MAIL
FANS@SHARONESTHERLAMPERT.COM

MOMMY
was my first fan to make **50X** of my poem. My fans are now making copies of my poems!

NAZI HUNTER Simon Weisenthal's Grandson made copies of my poem, **"A Survivor's Burden"** to hand out to his whole family!

LOVE OF MY LIFETIME
MOMMY EVE LAMPERT

(June 3, 1925-May 5, 1985)

At age 9, MOMMY was the only person in my life who knew who I was from the **INSIDE OUT!**

Tragically, she passed away at age 59 from breast cancer before all of my literary works were published.

She would make **50X** copies of each poem on her office copy machine. My **FANS** are now making **50X** copies.

MOMMY left this note on my desk in my bedroom before she left to work, and this note is published in every literary work.

Age 9
Darling Sharon,
THE QUEEN HAS ARRIVED!
My daugher is a poet, philosopher, and teacher.
My daugther is the Princess & the Pea!
BEAUTY & BRAINS!
Mommy,
XOXO

Unleash The Creator The GOD Within

FANS@SHARONESTHERLAMPERT.COM

Harry McVeety

A PHENOMENON...
SHARON ESTHER LAMPERT

Lithe and lovely ... like a fawn.
This lady fascinates me ... from dusk till dawn.
Feminine and comely ... she's beyond belief
A blue-beam from her eyes ... is my soothing relief.

Girlish in her braces ... maidenly in her style
I yearn for her embraces ... and adore her friendly smile.
As tasteful as any artist ... you'll ever see
She's a compendium of class ... from A to Z.

If you'd like to see a figure, that puts Venus to shame
Behold her in a swimsuit, and your passions will aflame.
Ever exuding goodness ... guided from above
Miss Sharon is the essence, and epitome of Love.

She's the inspiration of sages, and also fools like me
And the most magnificent female, I'm sure I'll ever see.
The nights are now endearing, & never filled with doubt
I sometimes wake up singing, cause it's Sharon ...
I dream about.

Affectionately,...
A devoted fan,
—Harry McVeety

V.E.S.S.E.L. Very. Extra. Special. Sharon. Esther. Lampert.

FANS@SHARONESTHERLAMPERT.COM

President of Fan Club: Rabbi David Posner

Congregation Emanu-El
of the City of New York
Fifth Avenue at Sixty-fifth Street
New York, N.Y. 10021-6596

Study of
DAVID M. POSNER

```
                                        June 17, 1998
                                        23 Sivan 5758

Dearest Sharon:

     I received your large and delightful envelope
today, with the poems which I had the pleasure of
reading last year -- but now mounted so beautifully.
Thanks for being so kind, thoughtful, and generous.

     I shared everything with Richie Chapin, because we
cannot get over you: Jewish mind, Jewish heart, Jewish
soul; brilliant, creative, athletic, serious, funny,
and gorgeous. I truly believe you are a super-woman.
But, most of all, I love your nick-name from the
Women's Minyan: Sharon Hag-bah-hah Lampert. This is
hysterical.

     God should lead you only in straight and good
paths.

     Put me down as President of your fan club.

                                    With deep affection,
```

Unleash The Creator The GOD Within

FAN MAIL
FANS@SHARONESTHERLAMPERT.COM

President of Fan Club: Rabbi David Posner

Congregation Emanu-El
of the City of New York
Fifth Avenue at Sixty-fifth Street
New York, N.Y. 10021-6595

Study of
DAVID M. POSNER

September 22, 1999

The New York Public Library
Humanities and Social Sciences Library
Fifth Avenue and 42nd Street
New York, NY 10018-2788

Dear Friends:

Sharon Esther Lampert has made application for a fellowship from the Center for Scholars and Writers. It is with greatest pleasure that I write to you in support of her application.

I can best describe this remarkable woman by citing the analysis of Moses Maimonides, in his "Guide for the Perplexed," concerning psychological endowments. He noted the class of people who are intellectually superior, but whose imaginative faculties are deficient. These, he said, were philosophers. Then there are those whose imaginative faculties are highly developed, but who are deficient intellectually. He said these are dreamers and politicians. But then he observed the rare people who have both highly developed intellects and imaginations. These, he said, are prophets.

Sharon Esther Lampert falls into the last category. She has one of the most gifted intellects I have ever encountered, and her imaginative capacity is absolutely awesome.

I have known many people throughout my long career at Temple Emanu-El. I have never met anyone like this extraordinary human being.

Again, awesome is the most appropriate word.

Yours truly,

FORMED BY THE CONSOLIDATION OF EMANU-EL CONGREGATION AND TEMPLE BETH-EL

FAN MAIL
FANS@SHARONESTHERLAMPERT.COM

Cody Howell, High School Student

Cody Howell
1042 Prospect Dr.
Imperial, Mo 63052
May 2, 2005

Sharon Esther Lampert
P.O.BOX 103,
New York, New York,10028,US

Dear, Sharon E. Lampert

Hello, My name is Cody, I am a Junior at Windsor High School in Missouri. I have had the chance to write to any one person and I picked you. I have always enjoyed quotes and sayings. Theirs just something about it, like I have always known there is a "better way" but never really found anything until I started to pay attention that their was more than just physical happenings. The poet has the ability to drink from streams science has yet to discover. I used to always reads one liners like
" a community begins to grow when old men plant trees they know they will never enjoy the shade of." Things like this really interested me. Something more than what I had known.

    I am very curious by nature, and this kind of wisdom/intellect really hit the spot for me, now I have many poems, sayings, quotes ext. I can't recite them by heart but I thouroulsy enjoyed the ones I read. I didn't know of you until me and my buddy were talking about how we like psychology and basically more than average and the "better way". After reading some of your quotes I realized you must have seen your share of happenings and become very wise over the years of thought, poetry, and life.

    My first thought was to write to you and try to flatter you because I enjoyed your work. Well I guess you made your poetry your work. Then I started thinking that this well of knowledge , all that stuff you've learned, it would be a long shot but my curiosity wouldin't stop unless if I asked you if you could share some of the knowledge you have gained. Any and all would be appreciated and probably useful later considering I am still just a 17-year-old kid. I can't think of any other word than greedy, but you have already thought so many with your influences, and I ask you to help me out, If your busy you have already done more than enough, thank you, and thanks for your time while reading this. I am sorry but I always find myself looking for more and I'm positive you have gained useful info in your day. I could imagine the child who has heard many stories, lesions, and wisdoms of many. He'd be one of the most diverse ,intelligent humans around, and with something like this in mind how could I not be greedy.

    I have already learned some from Internet, friends like the one who told me about poems, and family. I have tried to learn patience from the impatient, kindness from the angry, and truth from fools, but for some reason I'm not thankful for these teachers. I still feel as if I could have more, and the lessons of an older experienced poet just has something about how it sounds. Greatness is all I've seen come from poets their ability to make one think is amazing , I could just imagine the wisdom of an experienced one.

    Either way I just wanted to say thank you for your time and thank you for doing what you have done. Your shared wisdom and lessons will help many and your work might not be remembered forever but I believe that your positive effect will. Thank you again

    Your student ,
    Cody

#1 Poetry Website for Student Projects

Date: Thursday, November 19, 2009, 3:11 PM
Dear Ms. Lampert,
I am working on a poetry project for my senior English class. Instead of a boring research paper we are to analyze a famous poet and make a power point, and a creative presentation over the poets life, work and also criticisms of their work. The last part is the problem, I can't seem to find any scholarly criticisms of your work. Do you know of any, or have on record any criticisms of your work, either oral or written? My project partner and I would love to do our project on you because we find you very interesting and your poems very in tune with the lives of people today and the problems we face as modern people.
Any help would be appreciated.
Thank you again.
Sincerely,
Michael Rockey

Date: April 10, 2009 6:15:32 PM
Hi Sharon!
My name is Alexa & I'm a junior in high school! I love your poems, especially about world affairs. I will be doing a poetry analysis on three of your poems (I've chosen **Sandstorm in Iraq, Tsunami, and There Is No Flower in Darfur**) and also a presentation to inform the class of your works, accomplishments & biography. I have been searching every website and library on some information about you, but can't find any! If you can it would be greatly appreciated if you could tell me a little about your childhood, parents, education, religious beliefs, and maybe some experiences that have shaped your views or positions in regards to your poetry!
Thanks so much!
Have an amazing day!
Alexa Young

POETRY SEX SCANDAL
BARNES & NOBLE

BARNES & NOBLE
BOOKSELLERS

August 19, 2002

Sharon Esther Lampert
Kadimah Tribal Princess of Israel
P.O. Box 103
New York, NY 10028

Dear Sharon Esther Lampert:

Thanks for participating in our very successful monthly Open Mic hosted by Oreita Daley. Unfortunately, I have received complaints from customers attending the event regarding the erotica content of your poems, mentioning your commercial web site and passing out your poems and asking for audience participation.

The Open Mic is a program that was created to give as many poets as possible the opportunity to read and share their poetry with fellow poets and poetry lovers. Since the Open Mic takes place in a book store where customers are shopping, we ask the following:

Poets select material to read that is suitable for a general audience.

Poets be considerate of their fellow writers in choosing poems of appropriate length to read – so everyone has the opportunity to participate.

Poets should not pass out any kind of material including copies of poems or ask for audience participation.

Poets cannot promote their commercial web sites, products, services etc.

If you have any questions, please feel free to contact me directly.

Sincerely,

Frances Kelly
Frances Kelly
Community Relations Manager
Barnes & Noble
Upper E. Side (212) 794-2264

Read My Poetry Book: **Sweet Nothings: Portraits in Poetry**

Unleash The Creator The GOD Within
62

What Happens When You Dress Up Albert Einstein as Marilyn Monroe?
SHARON ESTHER LAMPERT

SEXIEST CREATIVE GENIUS IN HUMAN HISTORY

Kadimah Press: Gifts of Genius
Revelations! My Books Write Themselves!

18 Books of Poetry
Poet: The Greatest Poems Ever Written on Extraordinary World Events
Title: I Stole All the Words from the Dictionary
ISBN Hardcover: 978-1-885872-06-7
ISBN Paperback: 978-1-885872-07-4
ISBN E-Book: 978-1-885872-08-1

Prophet: WORLD PREMIERE!
Title: Who Knew God Was Such a Chatterbox
God Talks To Me: A Working Definition Of God
ISBN Hardcover: 978-1-885872-33-3
ISBN Paperback: 978-1-885872-34-0
ISBN E-Book: 978-1-885872-36-4

Prophet: WORLD PREMIERE!
Title: THE 22 COMMANDMENTS
All You Will Ever Need to know About **GOD**
A Universal Moral Compass For All Religions,
For All People, For All Time
ISBN Hardcover: 978-1-885872-03-6
ISBN Paperback: 978-1-885872-04-3
ISBN E-Book: 978-1-885872-05-0

Philosopher: WORLD PREMIERE!
Title: God of What? 10 Esoteric Laws of Inextricability
Is Life a Gift or a Punishment?
Measure the Pain! Measure the Pleasure!
ISBN Hardcover: 978-1-885872-00-5
ISBN Paperback: 978-1-885872-01-2
ISBN E-Book: 978-1-885872-02-9
GodofWhat.com

Prodigy: WORLD PREMIERE!
Title: Unleash the Creator The God Within
10 Esoteric Laws of Genius and Creativity
ISBN Hardcover: 978-1-885872-21-0
ISBN Paperback: 978-1-885872-22-7

No Fakes!
No Fat!
No Fluff!
No Filler!
No Flops!
No Flab!
NO Fudge!
No F-Bomb

All Global Bookstores

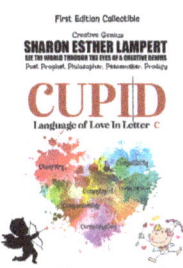

Prodigy: WORLD PREMIERE!
Title: CUPID: The Language of Love
—Written in Letter C
ISBN Hardcover: 978-1-885872-55-5
ISBN Paperback: 978-1-885872-56-2
ISBN E-Book: 978-1-885872-57-9
SharonEstherLampert.com

Popular: Children's Book, Ages 8-12
True Story of a Piano-Playing Cat
Title: SCHMALTZY:
In America, Even a Cat Can Have a Dream
ISBN Hardcover: 978-1-885872-39-5
ISBN Paperback: 978-1-885872-38-8
ISBN E-Book: 978-1-885872-37-1
Schmaltzy.com

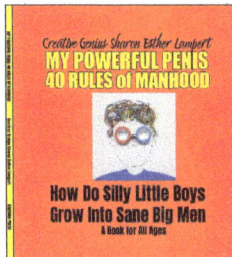

Popular: For Men of All Ages
Title: SILLY LITTLE BOYS
40 RULES OF MANHOOD
How Do Silly Little Boys Grow
into Big Sane Men?
14 Global Catastrophes of Violence
Against Women
ISBN Hardcover: 978-1-885872-29-6
ISBN Paperback: 978-1-885872-35-7
ISBN E-Book: 978-1-885872-41-8
SillyLittleBoys.com

Popular: Every Great Relationship
Begins with the Perfect Meal
Title: SEX ON A PLATE
FOOD AS FOREPLAY
The Cookbook of Everlasting Love
ISBN Hardcover: 978-1-885872-46-3
ISBN Paperback: 978-1-885872-48-7
ISBN E-Book: 978-1-885872-47-0
TrueLoveBurnsEternal.com

THANK YOU
Count Your Blessings. Practice Gratitude.

Blessing 1. **My Genetic Gift of Genius — Lefty**
- Genetic Inheritance: Two Sets of Artistic Genes: Painter Maternal Grandfather Benjamin Paikoff & Sculptor Father Abraham Lampert
- Vocalist: Ashira Orchestra (YOUTUBE video)
- Athlete: "Faster Than Any Boy, Anytime, Anywhere, Any Age!"

Blessing 2. My Life: Dawn of the Digital Revolution
- APPLE: Golden Age of Personal Computers
- ADOBE: Golden Age of Creativity
- INGRAM: Golden Age of Publishing
- SOCIAL MEDIA: Golden Age of Internet & Global Communication
- iTUNES: Golden Age of Music & Lyrics

NYU Professor Laurin Raiken

Blessing 3. My Loved Ones
- Self-Love: **M**indfulness, **M**editation, and **M**usic **M**itigates **MADNESS!**
- Unconditional Love: MOMMY Eve Paikoff Ifcher Lampert
- My PURRfect Children: SCHMALTZY and FALAFEL, Schmaltzy.com
- My METAphysical Sister, Poet Hannah Sezenes, "ELI, ELI"
- My Muse: Karl Bardosh "Friends First and Forever, and Family"
- 7 Practice Husbands, Artist & Muses, Dates, and NYC Night Life
- My Bubbe Esther Tulkoff, EstherTulkoff.com

NYU Professor Karl Bardosh

Blessing 4. My Education, Educators, and Awards (YOUTUBE videos)
- "A LIST" One of the World's Greatest Poets — #1 Poetry Website for Student Projects
- EDUCATION: Earned 3 Degrees from NYU: BA, MA, MA
- NYU MENTOR, Professor Laurin Raiken
- AWARD: NYU "Multi-Interdisciplinary Award" and MA Class Representative at Graduation
- NYC Rockefeller University, Publication: "Hyperphagia and Obesity Induced by Neuropeptide Y" — Lab of Dr. Sarah Leibowitz and Dr. Glen Stanley
- AWARD: 100-Year Scholarship Award Winner, Presented by NYC Mayor Edward Koch
- AWARD: Empire Science Scholarship Award Winner
- AWARD: Jerusalem Fellowship Award, Aish Hatorah, Israel
- AWARD: First Prize: Upper East Side Resident Writing Contest
- President of My Fan Club: Rabbi David Posner of Temple Emanu-El, NYC

Blessing 5. My Sports
- NYC Marathon
- Basketball: NYU Women's Varsity Basketball Team, Center
- Basketball: NYC Urban Professional League
- Skiing: Heavenly, Lake Tahoe, Nevada
- Tennis: NYC Central Park Tennis Courts
- NYU Weightlifting Contest Winner! NYU Coles Sports Center I was the only contestant — so I won! (NYU Washington Square Newspaper)

NYU President Andrew Hamilton

Blessing 6. My Inspirations
- ISRAEL "AM YISRAEL CHAI!"
Lambs to Slaughter to **LIONS** and **LIGHT of the WORLD** — 22% of Nobel Prizes!
- NYC: The Golden Age of Personal Freedom & Creative Self-Expression

NYU President Lawrence Oliva

One of the World's Greatest Poets

http://famouspoetsandpoems.com/poets.html

Famous Poets and Poems   http://famouspoetsandpoems.com/poets

 Larry Levis (3) (1946 - 1996)

 Amy Levy (69) (1861 - 1889)

 Louise Labe (1) (1524 - 1566)

 David Lehman (58) (1948 - present)

 Jiri Mordecai Langer (1) (1894 - 1943)

 John Lindley (4) (1952 - present)

 Dimitris Lyacos (3) (1966 - present)

 Yahia Lababidi (10) (1973 - present)

 Laurie Lee (6) (1914 - 1997)

 Walter Savage Landor (52) (1775 - 1864)

 Michael Lally (1) (1942 - present)

 Major Henry Livingston, Jr. (23) (1748 - 1828)

 Roddy Lumsden (2) (1966 - present)

 Sharmagne Leland-St. John (5) (1953 - present)

 Sharon Esther Lampert (19) (0 - present)

M

 Claude McKay (76) (1889 - 1948)

 Spike Milligan (35) (1918 - 2002)

 Marianne Moore (18) (1887 - 1972)

 John Milton (102) (1608 - 1674)

 A. A. Milne (22) (1882 - 1956)

 Czeslaw Milosz (33) (1911 - 2004)

 Edgar Lee Masters (251) (1868 - 1950)

 William Matthews (10) (1942 - 1997)

 Edwin Muir (14) (1887 - 1959)

 Roger McGough (14) (1937 - present)

Walter de la Mare (44) (1873 - 1956)

Antonio Machado (8) (1875 - 1939)

Edna St. Vincent Millay (165) (1892 - 1950)

W. S. Merwin (23) (1927 - present)

John Masefield (25) (1878 - 1967)

Louis MacNeice (3) (1907 - 1963)

Thomas Moore (144) (1779 - 1852)

 Christopher Marlowe (6) (1564 - 1593)

WORLD FAMOUS QUOTES

LITERATURE IS POWERFUL BEYOND WORDS FOR IT CREATES WORLDS

SHARON ESTHER LAMPERT

FIGHT TO LIVE LIVE TO FIGHT BORN TO DIE

SHARON ESTHER LAMPERT

THERE IS ONLY ONE TRUTH NO ONE HAS THE TRUTH

SHARON ESTHER LAMPERT

LONELINESS IS DEATH SOLITUDE IS DIVINE

SHARON ESTHER LAMPERT

FAIR USE NOTICE

There are a few copyrighted materials whose use has not been specifically authorized by the copyright owner. We are making this material available in its efforts to advance the understanding of poetry, philosophy, spirituality, and education. We believe this constitutes a 'fair use' of the copyrighted material as provided for in Section 107 of the US Copyright Law.

South Florida Sun-Sentinel

DELRAY BEACH NEWS   PALM BEACH COUNTY NEWS

Spirituality workshop supports A Walk on Water fund

MARCI SHATZMAN MSHATZMAN@TRIBPUB.COM | JAN 20, 2016

Sharon Esther Lampert didn't bring her tiara when she moved here from New York, but she found one just in time to be one of the speakers at Barbara M. Wolk's second annual Spirituality Workshop Jan. 24.

"Barbara has this wonderful event in support of autistic children," said Lampert, an author, poet, philosopher and educator who plays a princess for her talks.

She expects to hand out her "30 Commandments: All You Ever Need to Know," at the workshop from 10:30 a.m. to 12:30 p.m. at the Shirley & Barton Weisman Community Center, 7091 W. Atlantic Ave., in Delray Beach.

Admission is a minimum of $10 and the event opens at 10 a.m. A live auction will include a sculpture called "Balance."

EVERY THOUGHT IN YOUR HEAD WAS PUT THERE BY A WRITER
SHARON ESTHER LAMPERT

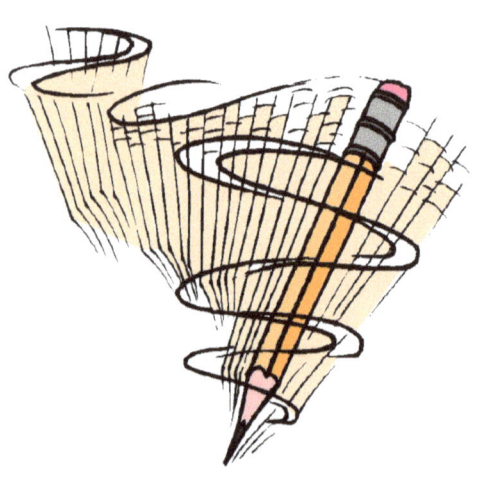

I Am Mortal.
My Books Are Immortal.
Please Handle My Books Gently.
My Books Are My Remains.

This book was compiled in six parts:
Part 1. Birth — April 15, 2014
Part 2. 10 Esoteric Laws — April 27, 2015
Part 3. Format Book — Jan 6, 2021
Part 4. 10 Essays — April 22-25, 2022
Part 5. Publish — August 8, 2022
Part 6. Update — July 7, 2023

Sharon Esther Lampert
SEE THE WORLD THROUGH THE EYES OF A CREATIVE GENIUS
Poet, Prophet, Philosopher, Peacemaker, Princess and Pea, Prodigy

www.ingramcontent.com/pod-product-compliance
Lightning Source LLC
Chambersburg PA
CBHW041319110526
44591CB00021B/2844